how to raise and train a pedigreed or mixed breed puppy

by Arthur Liebers

Distributed in the U.S.A. by T.F.H. Publications, Inc., 211 West Sylvania Avenue, P.O. Box 27, Neptune City, N.J. 07753; in England by T.F.H. (Gt. Britain) Ltd., 13 Nutley Lane, Reigate, Surrey; in Canada to the book store and library trade by Clarke, Irwin & Company, Clarwin House, 791 St. Clair Avenue West, Toronto 10, Ontario; in Canada to the pet trade by Rolf C. Hagen Ltd., 3225 Sartelon Street, Montreal 382, Quebec; in Southeast Asia by Y.W. Ong, 9 Lorong 36 Geylang, Singapore 14; in Australia and the south Pacific by Pet Imports Pty. Ltd., P.O. Box 149, Brookvale 2100, N.S.W., Australia. Published by T.F.H. Publications, Inc. Ltd., The British Crown Colony of Hong Kong.

ACKNOWLEDGMENTS

The photographs in this book were taken by Three Lions, Inc. and Louise Van der Meid with the cooperation of the best kennels in the world.

ISBN 0-87666-370-6

CONTENTS

These Fox Terrier puppies would fit easily into most any home, whether in the city or country. This breed's outgoing personality and compact size make them very popular housepets.

When selecting your puppy, try to match the dog to yourself and your family. Take care to select a dog that appears healthy and spirited.

1. Choosing Your Puppy

Actually, this chapter should be called "Letting Your Puppy Choose You." In real life, it is the puppy that does the choosing, except in the case of professional breeders or dog exhibitors who pick their dogs on the basis of blood-lines and champions. When the ordinary prospective dog buyer visits a kennel or pet shop, one of the little animals looks up at him with soulful eyes or licks his hand, and the person is "sold."

While most dogs and people can manage to get along together after the period of initial adjustment, there are far too many mismatings in which the wrong person and the wrong type of dog get together. You can reduce mismating possibilities by planning your dog acquisition in advance.

LET'S LOOK AT DOGS

A purebred dog is a type of dog that is recognized by the American Kennel Club as a distinct breed. The greatest advantage in choosing a purebred puppy is that you know what the dog will be like in appearance, size and behavior when he grows up. The cute, cuddly mixed breed puppy that you select at random may grow into a big, long-haired pony-sized animal when what you really wanted was a small pet. The long-legged mixed breed puppy that you visualize as a large-sized companion for country walks may stop growing soon and turn out to be a small house-loving pet.

When you buy a purebred puppy, you will be reasonably certain of having that kind of dog when the puppy has matured. Purebred dogs vary very little in size, conformation, weight and other physical traits. In addition, dogs of a particular breed usually have definite temperament and behavior characteristics.

Which is the best breed? There is no answer to that question. The information in this chapter may help you decide which is the best breed for *you,* or it may turn out that you'd be happier with the mixed breed or mongrel dog that happens to strike your fancy.

SORRY, IT ISN'T SO

Dog choosing is confused by a number of old wives' tales about dogs that just don't fit the facts. Purebred dogs are not more nervous than mixed breeds. Mongrels aren't smarter than purebreds. Female dogs are not always more home-loving and affectionate than males. Long-haired dogs do not shed more around the house than short-haireds.

THE CASE FOR THE MIXED BREED DOG

Just as many Poodle fanciers think Poodles are the only dogs to have, and Boxer owners think their dogs are head and withers above all others, the owner of the indiscriminate mixed breed puppy will defend his choice with equal vigor.

The initial outlay of money, of course, is much less for puppies of unknown ancestry. Although they require the same inoculations and diet as dogs with an established family tree, their masters often argue that they are less expensive to maintain because they stay healthier than highly bred animals. This is a controversial point, and if it is true that the vet's waiting room has fewer mongrels sitting around, it may only be because mongrel owners are less likely to panic at a sniffle.

Mixed breed dogs can be trained to do anything a purebred dog can do. The element of surprise in a mixed breed dog is also appealing to many. Who knows what that little mound of fur will grow into? Every day brings a new development as the puppy gradually becomes a dog, unlike any other. For mongrels are indeed unique, with no two looking exactly alike. This makes them good conversation pieces, for their owners are constantly asked by strangers, "What kind of dog is that?" (The tone of voice in which the question is asked determines the answer.)

SOME DOG CHOOSING FACTS

There are some facts that you should consider if you are going about the business of dog selection on a level-headed basis. One is the matter of initial expense. You can obtain a mixed breed dog that will make a perfectly satisfactory pet for a very few dollars. A run-of-the-mill specimen of a purebred type will cost at least $25 or $30 and may run into several hundred for one of the more popular breeds with championship potentials. If you have a poodle or one of the other breeds that require constant clipping, you are adding another item of expense.

Feeding a dog is largely a matter of providing food per pound of dog. A Great Dane or St. Bernard is bound to make a big dent in your weekly food budget. A small dog can be kept healthy on a very small outlay for dog food.

WHICH ONE OF THE 122?

The 122 different breeds of purebred dogs are divided into six groups, based on the original purpose for which the dogs were bred and what they are being used for today. Knowing the different groups may help you decide which group you'd like your dog to come from, and will narrow down your choice to a smaller number of breeds.

Group One, the Sporting Group, consists of breeds which are used to hunt and to retrieve water and land fowl. These dogs seem to have an instinctive interest in birds. In this group are the Setters, Pointers, Retrievers, Spaniels and Weimaraners.

The Hounds make up Group Two. These are dogs which were originally bred to trail fur-bearing animals. They are characterized by a keen sense of smell and are mostly fast-moving dogs. As in the other goups, the hounds are found in various sizes, from the low-slung Dachshunds to the huge Wolfhounds. Other hounds are the Afghans, Beagles, Bassets, Greyhounds and Whippets.

The Working Group, Group Three, includes the dogs whose original duty was to guard their master and assist him in his daily work. They are herders, guard dogs, sled dogs and others whose main function was to do a dog's job, although today they are primarily pets. In this group are the Boxers,

Collies, Dobermans, Great Danes, the small Corgis, Huskies, St. Bernards, German Shepherds and others.

The Fourth Group, the Terriers, were the rodent catchers of their early breeders, and are usually smaller, spunky dogs, although a few in this group are large in size. They include the Airedales, Bull Terriers, Fox Terriers, Yorkshire Terriers, Irish Terriers, Miniature Schnauzers, Scottish Terriers, Sealyhams, Bedlingtons and similar breeds.

For a pocket-sized dog, you'll find your choice in Group Five, the Toy Dogs. Many of these are miniature replicas of the larger breeds. Some of the currently popular "toys" are the Chihuahuas, Toy Spaniels, Toy Poodles, Miniature Pinschers, Pugs, Maltese and Pekingese.

A catch-all assortment of breeds is found in Group Six, called the Non-Sporting Group. Poodles (standard and miniature), Boston Terriers, Bulldogs, Dalmatians and other breeds that don't seem to fit into any of the other five groups meet here.

These three Dachshund puppies have alert eyes and healthy coats, signs that they have received proper care and nutrition. Dachshund fanciers have worked hard to maintain the breed exactly as nature first produced it and these dogs are still among the most popular of all breeds.

These cute little puppies would entice any prospective buyer, but consider the grown dog first. In a year or so these puppies will be over 60 pounds of Boxer requiring adequate space and exercise. Will they fit in with your lifestyle?

WHAT ABOUT SIZE?

The largest breeds, Great Danes, Irish Wolfhounds, St. Bernards and Newfoundlands need plenty of room. Aside from these dog "monsters," other large dogs can live happily in a small apartment if they get enough exercise. In fact, many apartment dwellers find that a larger dog is preferable to a small dog, because the larger dogs are uually less active than the smaller breeds and not so noisy. Small dogs seem to come equipped with a built-in barking mechanism that keeps active. (If a barking dog would mean trouble with the neighbors or the landlord, the Basenji is a good dog which cannot bark. It is also possible to have a veterinarian perform a relatively inexpensive operation to silence any dog's barking apparatus.)

PUPPY VS. GROWN DOG

Above all, keep in mind that all puppies, like all babies, are adorable and appealing. You are never buying a puppy, you are really buying a potential adult dog. Keep that adult dog in your mind's eye when you go dog shopping; and perhaps you'd be even better off buying an older dog. You'll miss a lot of the thrills of enjoying your dog's puppyhood with him—you'll also miss the hard work that goes into bringing up a puppy.

If you have small children in your family, you should consider them as important factors in dog buying. Small kids are tough on a young puppy. Young children are far better off with a medium- or larger-sized dog that is strong enough to stand the buffeting that a dog takes from the juvenile members of the family. In addition, a quiet, larger dog is less liable to snap back at a child in self-defense than a smaller, more excitable dog.

When considering which puppy is best for your family, take into account the amount of care that the dog's coat will require to keep it in top condition. Most long-haired dogs require daily grooming to prevent matting and snarling, while the short-haired dogs need relatively little grooming and will do well with just an occasional brushing to remove dead hairs. A beautifully long, silky coat requires both good health in the dog and a conscientious grooming plan carried out by the dog's owner.

LONG-HAIRED VS. SHORT-HAIRED

Some people like dogs with long hair; others prefer short hair; some may find themselves happier with the Mexican hairless dog. Long hair means more work because the dog must be groomed and brushed and a long-haired dog may develop a "doggy" smell unless he is groomed frequently. On the "for" side, the long-haired dog won't need a blanket in cold climates. If the lady of the dog-acquiring household is on the finicky side, consider that short-haired dogs will shed more hair on furniture and clothing. One of the few non-shedders is the Poodle. And let's not avoid unpleasant possibilities. Dogs *do* acquire fleas and ticks, and it's easier to keep a short-haired dog free of these little pests.

HOW TO KNOW A HEALTHY PUPPY

Puppies—in fact adult dogs too—spend much of their time sleeping. The fact that the puppy you are viewing is sleepy is not a bad sign, but try to avoid making your first visit to him (or her) shortly after the feeding period.

A healthy puppy should be frisky, should have a good, smooth coat, bright eyes and a friendly disposition. Beware of the puppy that has a running nose, eyes that discharge pus, or diarrhea.

Most pet shops or kennels will allow you to take the puppy to a veterinarian for a health check-up with the privilege of return if the vet vetoes the animal. Usually they'll require a note in writing from the vet.

MALE OR FEMALE?

Here again it's a matter of personal preference. The male may be a little harder to housebreak; the female will require special care for a few weeks during the year when she is in "heat." In many breeds the males are a bit larger and stronger than the female; some male dogs may tend to roam more than females. Females can be bred—although the amateur dog owner who plans to make a profit on breeding his dog is usually doomed to disappointment. Spaying the female will eliminate the possibility of breeding and also the "heat" periods, but the cost of the operation may be about $30.00.

TALK TO PEOPLE FIRST

People in the dog world, professional trainers, kennel owners, pet shop operators, all like to talk about dogs. If you have never had a dog before, talk over the situation with some "experts" first. They'll be able to give you facts about the temperaments of the different breeds and just how much time and effort dog owning will involve on your part. There are also good books about each breed. It may be unfortunately true that you shouldn't have a dog. Some people and families just aren't geared to dog owning and it's best to find out first.

This beautiful family of Collies shows different color inheritance patterns, three of the puppies resemble their blue-merle colored mother while one puppy is a tri-color like the sire.

2. Registration and Pedigrees

REGISTRATION

Now, let's look into the confusing business of a puppy's papers. Assuming that you buy a purebred dog, you will want the necessary papers to prove that he is a true representative of his breed. If he is eligible for registration papers from the American Kennel Club, both his parents must have been registered in the A.K.C. as purebred dogs.

If the litter in which your puppy was born was registered with the A.K.C., then your puppy was given a name under which he was registered. The seller gives you the Registration Certificate. On the back is a transfer form which you must fill out and send in to the American Kennel Club at 51 Madison Avenue, New York, N.Y. 10010, with a fee of $1.00 to have your self registered as the new owner of the dog.

On this Registration Certificate, you find the name of your puppy, his breed, color and any markings, the name and registration numbers of his sire and dam (dog terms for father and mother), the sex of the puppy, date of birth and name of the breeder.

This inquisitive looking Basset Hound already shows signs of the sturdy, powerfully built dog it will someday be.

If the litter has not been registered individually, you should receive an Application for Registration form, giving the same information but with a blank space for the name of the puppy and for your name as its owner. This must be signed by the breeder. Fill in your name and address and the name you select for your puppy and send it to the American Kennel Club with the $4.00 registration fee, and in a few weeks you will receive (if the name you have chosen for the puppy is approved) your Registration Certificate with your puppy's registration number.

PEDIGREE

The Pedigree is the family tree of your puppy, and is not part of his official registration papers. If you are interested in breeding for sale or are planning to enter your dog in shows, then the Pedigree is of interest because it will show how many of your puppy's ancestors have won their championships in the show ring or in obedience competition.

The letters "Ch." before a dog's name on a Pedigree indicate that it is a breed champion. Letters after the dog's name indicate obedience degrees that the dog has won. For example, Fido, C.D. means that the dog has won the first obedience degree of Companion Dog; C.D.X. stands for the second degree, Companion Dog Excellent; U.D. for Utility Dog, the highest obedience title. The letter "T" after the dog's name means that it has qualified as a Tracking Dog.

If the breeder of your dog doesn't have the Pedigree you can have one drawn up by the kennel club with which your puppy is registered for a few dollars. The amount charged depends on how many generations back you want the pedigree traced.

Naturally, the more champions in a dog's background the more expensive it may be; and its puppies will be that much more valuable.

LICENSING

Registering your puppy does not take the place of the license which is required by the local county or city authorities. Fees vary in different states and within states. Some charge more for a female than a male. For information on obtaining a license – which is usually required for dogs over 6 months of age – call the local chapter of the A.S.P.C.A., your police department or your town clerk's office.

The license tag which you receive will serve to identify your dog if he is lost and it's also a good idea to have a tag made with your name, address and phone number to hang on the dog's collar. In addition to the license, in some areas, the dog must wear a tag showing that he has been inoculated against rabies.

3. Feeding Your Puppy

Puppies are usually sold when they are from 5 or 6 weeks to 4 months of age. Most puppies are weaned when they are about 5 weeks old and at that age they are ready to begin feeding themselves. Before you take your puppy home, ask what he has been eating so that you can keep him on the same diet for a while, as a change will be liable to upset his digestive system.

Remember that a puppy is basically a baby animal, not a human baby. His wild ancestors have provided him with a powerful digestive system. Dogs gulp their food; they do not chew like well-mannered little children. Most puppies will overeat if they have the opportunity; and their little stomachs will promptly reject the food, so don't get excited if your puppy sometimes sends back a meal. Vomiting isn't serious unless it becomes a regular thing after each meal.

Until your puppy is about 4 months old, he should get 4 meals a day, stretched over a 12-hour period, about 4 hours apart. He can have his first meal when you get up in the morning.

FOUR-MEAL DIET

For breakfast, give your puppy as much milk (or diluted evaporated milk) as he wants, slightly warmed to take the chill out of it, but not boiled. Add to the milk a few spoonsful of pablum or other breakfast cereals. A few times a week hard boil an egg, break it into small pieces, and throw it into his breakfast dish. Mix in a spoonful of an animal vitamin powder or liquid. The one-dish meal may look a little messy to you, but your puppy will enjoy it.

Four hours later, lunchtime has arrived. This calls for a meat dish. You can use one of the canned dog foods or chopped meat. If you buy meat, get the cheaper kind of chopped hamburger meat because it contains more fat. If you use canned dog food, add some beef fat to it. Try feeding the meat raw and cooked to see which the puppy prefers. Add to meat or canned food enough warm water to make a soupy mix, then add enough kibble (baked crumbled dog biscuit) or puppy meal to absorb most of the water. As to amount, you can follow the directions on the food packages or work by trial and error. Don't leave food lying around all day. Give the puppy 10 or 15 minutes to finish his meal, then remove it.

Another 4 hours and it's feeding time again. Now, repeat the breakfast menu.

Some time around 8 o'clock in the evening give the puppy his final meal of the day, which should be another meat meal, the same as his midday feeding. However, cut down a bit on the liquid content of the final meal. (This will tie in with the housebreaking training that will be going on.)

This is a sample menu, not one that you have to follow. Many dogs are perfectly healthy and have never tasted meat in their lives. You can start your puppy on a kibble diet, soaking the biscuit fragments in a meat or vegetable soup to make them more tempting. If you have a large family, chances are that you can find enough "leavings" to keep your puppy contentedly fed.

The puppy himself will give you the best indication whether or not his diet is satisfactory. If he is plump, shiny coated and active, and his bowel droppings are firm and not watery, then you're doing fine in the puppy feeding department.

At about 4 months of age, you can eliminate one of the daily feedings. For breakfast, give milk, cereal and egg. At noontime and again about 4 or 5 o'clock provide a meal of meat, puppy meal or kibbled biscuit, and add any green cooked vegetables from the family table. If the puppy seems to be hungry at bedtime, let him have a few small dry dog biscuits.

Commercially canned dog foods are highly recommended to supplement dry dog chows since they are fortified with necessary vitamins and minerals to make the food nutritionally complete.

The abundance of skin on this Bloodhound puppy is a good indicative sign that he will grow into a dog having the desirable breed trait of extremely loose skin which hangs in deep folds.

"NO" TO THESE

Most dogs will not react well to pork. Keep the dog away from chicken or small meat bones that may splinter. Don't give a young dog candies, cakes, white bread or too many starchy foods. Green peas may give your dog gas; almost all other cooked vegetables are good for him. Don't get your dog in the habit of eating expensive cuts of meat. The cheaper kinds of meat which contain fat and some gristle are really much better for him. Besides a dog may become a finicky eater if he has been spoiled.

FEEDING THE OLDER PUPPY

When he gets to be about 7 months old, the average puppy becomes a little fussy about his eating. If he is in good, plump condition, you can cut him down to two meals a day, dropping the noon feeding, and increasing the size of the evening meal. At this time, take a firm stand on his diet. A dog is smart enough to figure out that if he refuses his own food he will get the better-tasting table leftovers. The owner has to be smarter. It won't hurt a dog to go hungry until he learns that he has to eat what he is served in his own food dish. Once you give in and let him spurn his dog food for sirloin from the table, you've started trouble for yourself.

Handouts from the dinner table are good for your dog and should be used as a treat. It may be hard to resist the appealing "I'm-starving-to-death-and-you're-eating-steak" look, but just as Junior learned to eat spinach to get dessert, your dog has to learn to eat his own food when it's placed in front of him.

REFUSING TO EAT

Occasionally a puppy or older dog will refuse a meal. Sometimes a dog will get fed up with the same old menu, but he'll eat the meal if you do something to add a different taste to his dish. Pour in a few tablespoons of soup, or a bouillon cube, or a few scraps of seasoned meat from your own food. Or, it may be that the animal just isn't hungry. Take away the food, put it in the refrigerator, warm it and serve it for the next meal.

Of course, if your dog persistently refuses to eat, there may be some reason for it and a visit to the vet may be needed. Some of the smaller breeds, particularly Dachshunds, will sometimes go on a hunger strike for several days for no good reason. Sometimes the food refusal is just a bid for attention; the puppy or dog will eat the food if you hand it to him, mouthful by mouthful – but don't let your dog get into the habit of demanding plate-to-mouth service. A little hunger never hurt a healthy dog.

You should feed your puppy at regular hours in clean dishes and remove the dishes as soon as he has eaten. A newspaper placed under the dishes will prevent drippings.

RAW MEAT, COOKED MEAT, OR NO MEAT?

As soon as you begin taking your puppy out for walks, you will run into other dog owners and discover that almost everyone at the end of a leash is an "expert" on dog feeding and that no two agree. Some will assure you that raw meat makes a dog vicious and gives him worms; others that cooking meat kills all the vitamins; still others will say that their dog has been raised on some brand of dog food and never tasted meat.

Dogs are carnivorous, which means that meat is their natural food. The older puppy should receive from ¼ pound of meat to a pound or more daily, depending on the dog's size and his activity. The young puppy's meat should ground or chopped; for the older puppy, the meat may be cut into chunks about the size of a golf ball, or he may be given ground meat. As to cooking meat, that should depend on whether or not you have the time to cook it; it doesn't seem to make much difference to the animal. However, if your dog has loose bowels and has been eating raw meat, giving him cooked meat for a few days may help.

The commercial kibble biscuits on the market contain a large proportion of meat products and your dog can be raised on them satisfactorily. For the sake of economy and variety, many find that mixing meat and

This charming Corgi pup illustrates the alert, foxy expression that is so characteristic of the breed.

biscuit or meal about half-and-half with warm water or soup makes a satisfactory diet for the dog, and the budget.

Beef is probably the most nutritious for the dog, but lamb or mutton can be fed. Almost any meat product that's lowest in cost at the time will serve for the puppy's food. If you check the contents on the labels of canned dog food, you'll find that they include liver, hearts, kidneys, lungs, poultry parts and tripe.

There is no reason to go out into the rain or snow at 6 o'clock in the morning because you find that the dog's food supply has been depleted. If you haven't any dog biscuit or meal, you can feed shredded wheat, toast or whole wheat bread. While a dog that's fed too much starch may get overfat and develop skin troubles, a moderate amount of spaghetti, macaroni and boiled potatoes won't harm him and will be enjoyed. However, try to avoid over-spicy foods. A tasty spaghetti sauce is too spicy for the dog

With plenty of good food, exercise and room to grow, this German Shepherd puppy should grow to be as healthy and hearty a specimen as his mother.

and will make him thirsty; he'll drink too much and you may have an "accident" in the house a few hours later.

In fact, almost anything that you eat won't hurt your dog. Rice, cheeses, eggs can all go into his food dish. On the vegetable side, throw him any cooked green vegetables, mashed carrots, etc.

ADD FAT TO HIS DIET

Perhaps the one food that most pet dogs do not get enough of is fat. The dog needs fat all year round to keep his skin and coat in condition, in summer as well as in winter. If you use horse meat for your dog's meat requirements, then be certain to add some beef fat (you can get all you need by asking your butcher for scraps) or bacon drippings to his food. If you notice any thin spots on your puppy's coat it may be a sign that he needs more fat in his diet; also added fat may cure a dry, scaly coat.

WATER, WATER EVERYWHERE

A pan of water should always be available to the puppy. When the dog knows he can have a drink any time he wants it, he will drink frequently, a little at a time. If you just produce water at intervals, the puppy will overdrink and may become sick, and it will be harder to teach him to control his tendency to leave puddles around.

If you notice that your dog is drinking an excessive amount of water, it may be a sign that something is wrong. Unusual thirst is one symptom of a number of dog ailments, and calls for a visit to the vet.

And, be especially careful to keep your dog's water dish 100% clean. Rinse it out a few times before refilling it, and if you use detergents to clean it, be certain that all the suds are out before you fill it again. Many of the modern detergents cling to dishes and sudsy water isn't good for your puppy.

A STYLISH FIGURE FOR YOUR DOG

The young puppy should be plump, but after about 3½ or 4 months, the puppy fat should begin to disappear. The dog's hipbones and his ribs are the guide as to whether his weight is up to par – or above it. The hipbones and ribs should be well covered with flesh; the ribs should not be too sharply outlined. Of course, with a bushy-haired dog it's harder to tell, but you can feel under the fur for a light padding of flesh over the bones.

Keeping your dog on the thin side is best, as most dogs tend to get fat later in life and the young dog that starts off thin has a better chance for a longer, healthier life.

4. Grooming Your Puppy

As a dog owner, you have three responsibilities to your puppy. First, feeding him; second, grooming him; and third, training him.

Feeding and grooming are essential to the health of the puppy as well as to his appearance. By keeping the puppy's coat clean and healthy you can prevent many common skin troubles which afflict ungroomed dogs. Brushing your puppy removes dead hairs and stimulates the skin oil glands. This also helps to reduce shedding and makes the puppy more popular around the house. Moreover, it will remove the need for him to do so much scratching. Many puppies who are accused of having fleas are merely scratching to remove dead hairs.

While daily grooming is not necessary, the dog should be gone over at least two or three times each week. Many dog owners claim that a well-groomed dog seems to take pride in his personal appearance and assists by keeping himself cleaner.

YOUR GROOMING EQUIPMENT

A brush, comb and a pair of scissors are all you need for your dog's grooming. If you have one of the long-haired dogs, you'll need a brush with long, stiff bristles that will reach down to the undercoat. Often the long hair on the underside of the dog will become matted, and for that you may need a "carder" (similar to the carder that is used on fur coats), on oblong-shaped brush with short, bent wire bristles. Short-haired dogs are groomed with a brush that has short stiff bristles. A steel comb with round teeth is useful to comb out matted hair.

Every pet shop has a variety of grooming tools and the salesperson can help you select the proper equipment for your needs.

START YOUNG

You should start grooming your puppy when he is about 8 or 9 weeks old. He really doesn't need it yet, but if you start him early enough he will learn to accept being handled and groomed as part of a dog's life. Trying to groom an older dog that has never been groomed can call for the services of three strong men.

This Puli mother and pup need plenty of careful grooming to properly maintain the heavily corded coat that is associated with this working breed.

Have a regular time and place for the grooming so that the puppy will accept it as part of his routine. Most puppies or dogs will accept grooming with less fuss if they are placed on a table – although you can expect to have your hands full the first few times. Most puppies will struggle and complain until they find out that they're not being hurt. (Have you ever taken a baby to the barber for his first haircut?)

HOW TO GROOM YOUR PUPPY

At first confine your grooming to brushing your puppy's hair until it is sleek and shiny. As the puppy grows older and gets around more, add the other items of grooming.

Use the scissors to trim away the hair between the toes, to remove any mats under the stomach or under the ears and to trim off any loose hairs that give the puppy an untidy look.

These lovely Scottish Terriers must be clipped and groomed at regular intervals to keep their coat in the traditional Scottie style.

If you have a Poodle, it's best to have his "puppy" cut administered by a professional groomer using an electric clipper; clipping should be repeated every two months or so. (For clipping instructions, see "How to Raise and Train a Poodle".)

Terriers are "stripped" two or three times a year – also a job calling for professional help. Other breeds should be combed and brushed regularly. While there's a difference of opinion about trimming down long-haired dogs during the summer in warmer climates, many experts now feel that the coat should be left alone as it helps protect him from the heat of the sun.

CHECK HIS COAT

Whenever you groom your dog, especially in warmer weather, check his coat for fleas, lice and ticks. With newly-developed insecticides it is not necessary to bathe your dog in order to free him of the first two types

If your puppy spends much time out of doors, examine his paws for burrs and other objects that may lodge between his toes or in his pads.

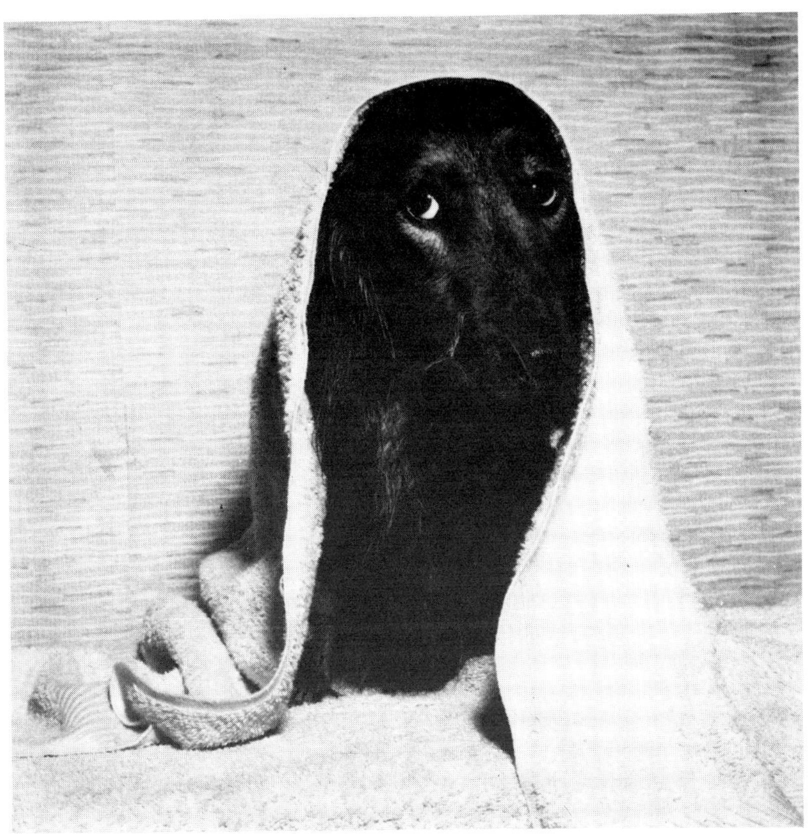

After the bath your puppy must be thoroughly dried with a heavy towel and kept warm.

of pests. Your veterinarian or your pet shop can provide you with powders that are highly effective against fleas or lice and will discourage ticks. However, read the instructions on the package carefully and follow them. Most should be kept out of the dog's eyes and you should wash your hands with soap and water immediately after using to prevent your own skin from absorbing the powder.

If you live in an area where ticks abound, check your puppy daily for these small blood-sucking insects. When you find a tick, lift it off, using a tweezer. First apply a dab of iodine or alcohol which will make the tick loosen its hold. Make sure that you get the whole tick off, and when you do apply a lighted match to it to kill it.

When you have found fleas, lice or ticks on your dog, immediately disinfect his sleeping quarters, using the same powder you used on the animal, and air out or change his bedding.

TO BATHE OR NOT TO BATHE

Many attractive-looking dogs have never had a bath in their lives. Others are plunged into a bath every time the sensitive nose of their owner detects the slightest whiff of a "doggy" odor. Some believe that too much bathing is bad for the natural oil in a dog's coat, and a dog can catch cold if he is bathed in cold weather and allowed to run outdoors before he is fully dry.

However, every dog at some time or other will get himself into some kind of smelly mess and need a good washing. When you bathe a puppy take precautions to keep him warm and dry him thoroughly after his bath. When bathing a puppy, his ears should be stuffed with cotton or lamb's wool, and a drop of caster oil should be dropped in each eye to protect it. If you are using a disinfectant in the water, be careful not to get any water in the dog's eyes. You can use any of the dog soaps that your pet shop has, or any mild, white soap on your dog, but be sure that all the soap is rinsed out of his coat. The dog will lick himself after his bath and soap left on him will very probably produce prompt vomiting.

Keen attention must be paid to the coats of these Yorkshire Terriers to keep them in good condition. Unlike most breeds, the Yorkie should be bathed frequently, usually twice a month, but be sure to protect the coat from drying out by using a lanolin-base shampoo.

Despite the beautiful white coat of the Great Pyrenees, this breed requires relatively little grooming and bathing to keep them in the best possible condition.

To check whether the coat is soapless, see whether it is shiny and "squeaks" when rubbed between your fingers.

If you find that bathing your dog is too much of a chore, you will find dry cleaners on the counter of your pet shop that will do a good job on your short-haired dog, and a liquid cleaner that works fine on long-haired breeds. Some even come in aerosol containers that you can squirt over your dog and rub out for a fast, effective cleaning.

For a do-it-yourself cleaning job, you can rub a few handfuls of corn meal into your dog's coat and brush it out.

OTHER GROOMING TIPS

While grooming your puppy, you should check his ears, nails and teeth. Too long nails can tear off or split and can cut the dog when he scratches himself. Using a nail clipper takes some skill and is best left to the veterinarian or the professional groomer. Most dogs will allow you to use a file on their nails without too much complaining. Get a fairly fine flat wood file and trim down the points of his nails. There's much less chance of trimming the nails too short if you use a file than if you try to use a clipper, which can cut a vein by mistake.

Remoxe wax and hairs from the ears with a tweezer and then swab out the ears with a piece of cotton dipped in alcohol, but be careful not to probe too far into the puppy's ears. Then, dry the ears and dust them with antiseptic powder – baby powder is fine for this.

For tooth care, wipe the puppy's teeth occasionally with a cloth dipped in a solution of salt water or in alcohol.

If your puppy is long-haired you may find that his eyes will "run" occasionally because hairs irritate the eyes and cause a discharge. For this, wash the eyes with any standard eyewash or with boracic solution; or your veterinarian may prescribe an ointment for this purpose.

NYLABONE® is a necessity that is available at your local petshop (not in supermarkets). The puppy or grown dog chews the hambone flavored nylon into a frilly dog toothbrush, massaging his gums and cleaning his teeth as he plays. Veterinarians highly recommend this product, but beware of cheap imitations which might splinter or break.

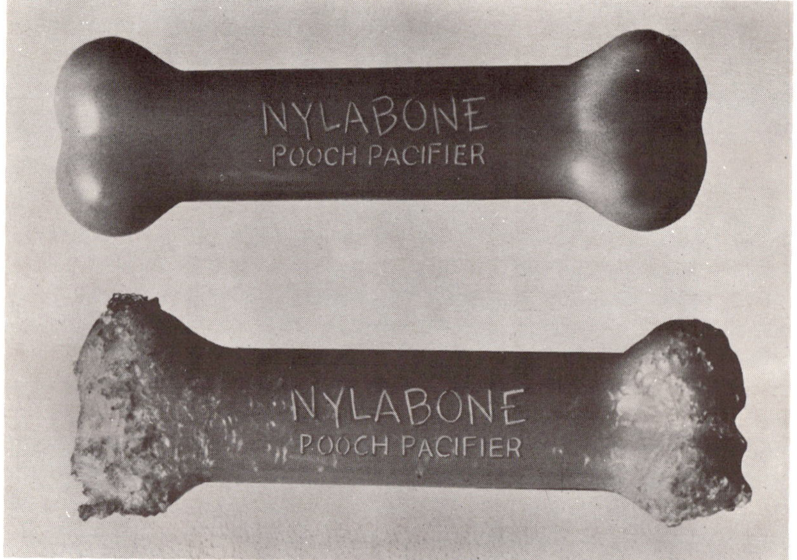

5. Your Puppy's Health

Are you a hypochondriac? If you are, your puppy will probably be traveling back and forth from the veterinarian every week. While there are times when a visit to the dog doctor is essential, a little common sense and a little knowledge will enable you to raise a healthy dog without causing you to apply for an income tax deduction for canine medical expenses. (You can't deduct them unless you are a professional dog breeder or kennel owner.)

First, and probably most important, keep the puppy clean. Provide him with clean sleeping quarters and wash and clean his food and drinking dishes. Keep him away from garbage, and off the street until he is a few months old.

INOCULATIONS ARE NECESSARY

When your puppy is 6 to 8 weeks old, he should begin to receive his distemper shots and he should get these about every two weeks until he is old enough for his "permanent" inoculation. The permanent inoculation is usually given when the puppy is 4 or 5 months old. A safe rule is to hold back the permanent inoculation until the second teeth have come in.

During the teething period, the puppy's resistance is low and some breeders have found that too early inoculation may have a poor effect on the puppy's permanent teeth. However, in this matter let your veterinarian be your guide. Most veterinarians give a three shot permanent inoculation at about 2- or 3-week intervals and a booster shot several months later. In addition, in many parts of the country an inoculation against rabies is required by law or is advisable, and another inoculation to protect against hepatitis may be recommended by your veterinarian.

KEEP HIM ISOLATED

A young puppy deserves as much protection against contagion as a young infant. Your puppy should not be exposed to a sick dog or be allowed to use an older dog's food dishes. Germs of infectious diseases may be carried on people's shoes or clothes and some may even be air-borne. Discourage over-handling of the young puppy and resist your own natural desire to show him off until he has a chance to build up resistance against the many dog diseases in the world.

This naturally active Silky Terrier puppy can find enough action around the house to keep him in good physical shape.

THE HELPFUL THERMOMETER

If you don't have one in the house, buy a rectal thermometer when you acquire a puppy. A healthy puppy's temperature should normally be about 102 degrees, although excitement can bring it up to 103 for a short time, and the business of having a glass tube stuck into his rear end can usually provide enough excitement to raise the temperature. However, any reading of over 103 degrees for any length of time shows that something is wrong and a veterinarian should be consulted.

Many of the dog's minor ailments are similar to human ailments – colds, coughs, upset stomachs, etc. The common-sense treatment before the doctor's visit should be very similar to that in treating a sick person. Keep the puppy quiet, don't feed him and don't give him any water for a while. To reduce the fever, give him aspirin – a baby-sized dose for a small dog, an adult dose for a larger dog.

It's fairly easy to give a puppy a pill. Hold his head tilted up, open his mouth, drop the pill into his throat and stroke his throat downwards until you feel him gulp. Watch him for a few minutes; some dogs will hold the pill in their mouth and then spit it out.

SIGNS OF SICKNESS

A dog can't tell you he's sick, but his appearance will often show it. A listless attitude, coughing, sneezing, continued refusal to eat, unusual thirst are among canine signs of illness. Almost all puppies will sometimes have diarrhea brought on by a change in diet, worms, or the onset of an illness. Sometimes a puppy will alternate between normal bowel movements and diarrhea.

Before getting excited over your puppy's diarrhea, try curing it by diet. If you have been feeding raw meat, give him several meals of cooked meat; if you have been feeding cooked meat, give him kibbled biscuits or other food. Another good anti-diarrhea food is cottage cheese. Replace the meat part of his meal with cottage cheese for a day. Also, instead of plain drinking water, give barley water or oatmeal water. If the diarrhea still persists, then have your veterinarian check the puppy for worms or other ailment.

AVOID DAMPNESS

A number of dog owners feel that the cellar or the garage is the place for the dog. That's all right if the cellar or garage is dry and well-ventilated. But dogs can catch pneumonia or a condition similar to arthritis from living in damp quarters. Your puppy or dog can live outdoors in almost any climate if he is given the chance to develop a resistance to cold. Outdoor-living dogs will usually grow a heavier coat than apartment or house dogs.

CAR SICKNESS

If you acquaint your puppy with car riding at an early age, he'll be less liable to get sick while out riding. A 6- to 8-week-old puppy will seldom get car sick, although an older dog may. Frequently, taking the dog out for an

Children in the family can do their part to keep the family pet clean and happy.

automobile ride *before* he is fed will forestall any bad effects. In many cases, car sickness is due to excitement and giving the dog a dose of sedative or any one of the human seasickness remedies may help.

In some cases, the cure is to associate the car with something pleasant in the puppy's mind. Sit him in a standing car and feed him there. Watch the puppy during his first auto rides. If he begins to act uneasy or to drool, then stop the car and take him out for a short walk.

Be sure that the dog has plenty of air and that he can look around him and see what's happening. Some dogs are more affected by car fumes than humans are and a leaking muffler or tailpipe may be letting fumes into the car that sicken the animal.

WORMING YOUR DOG

Almost every puppy will need to be wormed. The worms may be found in the puppy at birth – picked up from the mother – or the puppy may eat worm eggs from the floor or in his sleeping quarters.

There is no basis to the common belief that feeding a dog garlic will cure him of worms. There are five different types of worms and recognizing the type of infestation and curing it is a job for the veterinarian. Each of the five types requires different medicine and different treatment.

SYMPTOMS OF WORMS

The symptoms that indicate worm infestation may also be caused by other conditions. The coat may be dull, the skin dry and scaly and the puppy's eyes may have a dull look. Sometimes the puppy will drag his rear end along the ground – although this may be due to swollen anal glands (more about that later). A wormy dog may be thin with poor appetite, although one with tapeworm may be fat and overly hungry. Almost all types of worms cause diarrhea.

TYPES OF WORMS

The most prevalent in puppies is the roundworm which is 3 to 4 inches long and has a round, hard body. These are clearly seen in the puppy's stool and often are vomited up by the infested puppy.

The segments of tapeworm that you may find in the puppy's stool are like grains of rice in appearance, about ¼ inch to ½ inch long. Some may be found sticking to the dog's hair under his tail. These segments are pinkish-white when first passed out, but turn brown as they dry.

Eggs of the tapeworm are carried by lice and fleas and chances are that if the dog is heavily infested by these, he'll have tapeworm as well.

Whipworm and hookworm are almost invisible, being about the size of a fine hair. They can be detected only by microscopic examination of the puppy's stool. The whipworm lives in a blind-alley of the dog's intestine, similar to the human appendix, and an operation similar to an appendectomy is sometimes necessary to eliminate these worms. The hookworm lives in the dog's intestine and drains his vitality.

The heartworm, which lives in the dog's heart, lays eggs which circulate throughout his blood stream. It is not common except in parts of the South. The larvae of this worm are carried by mosquitoes, ticks and lice – more reason to keep your puppy clean of these pests.

TREATMENT FOR WORMS

Almost every puppy will need a worming when he is about 4 or 5 weeks old and again at about 6 months of age. Safest procedure is to let your

If you have small children in your family, be sure to choose a puppy that is sturdy enough to withstand the antics of a playful child.

veterinarian handle the worming. If you do it yourself, follow the directions on the bottles of worm capsules carefully and give worm medicines on an empty stomach. Do not worm a sick dog; after worming, feed the dog a rich diet with some vitamin supplement added.

BRONCHITIS

Loss of appetite, shivering, listlessness and a dry, racking cough are signs that your puppy has bronchitis. This may happen if he has been chilled after his bath, stayed in a drafty place, or slept where a fan or air conditioner has chilled him. The treatment is pretty much the same as the treatment for a child with a bad cold. Keep the puppy warm. If the weather is warm and sunny he can be allowed to bask in the sun. If the older puppy must be taken out for his walk in bad weather, wrap a piece of blanket around him if he hasn't a sweater.

If constipation accompanies the bronchitis, give him a dose of milk of magnesia — about a teaspoonful — or some mineral oil or castor oil. If the veterinarian isn't available you can find at your pet shop dog cough medicine and terramycin or other antibiotics especially prepared for animals.

Sometimes the symptoms of bronchitis are accompanied by diarrhea. If that happens give the puppy a teaspoonful of Kaopectate every four hours until the diarrhea ceases.

CONSTIPATION

Constipation, with no other symptoms, is usually the fault of improper feeding and can be remedied by changing the diet. Add more vegetables to the puppy's diet; increase the amount of roughage — dog biscuits and meal — in his diet, cut down on the amount of milk you have been giving him. If the condition persists, give a teaspoonful of mineral oil.

EAR CANKER

Many long-haired, long-eared dogs, especially Cocker Spaniels, are liable to suffer from ear canker. If you find your puppy scratching and pawing his ears, examine them carefully. Looking inside the ear, you may find a brownish substance. Inside this dirt there are little mites that cause the dog considerable annoyance. Clean the dog's ear immediately with cotton dipped in olive oil and remove as much of the brown deposit as you can without hurting the animal. Then, obtain the special canker medication from your pet shop or veterinarian and use it as directed.

A dog's disposition may change because of the pain he suffers from ear canker. If your dog or older puppy shows a tendency to snap at anyone who pets his head or ears, check him for this condition before blaming him for being a vicious animal.

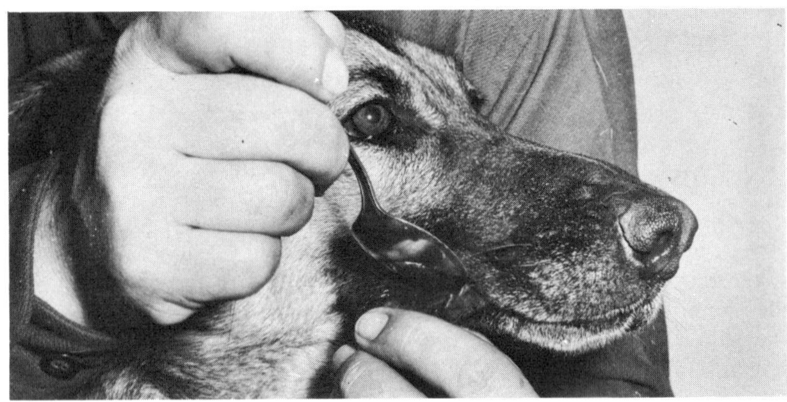

When giving liquid medicine, merely pour the liquid into his jowls. Then hold his head up so it will slip down into his throat and he will swallow it without losing any.

When giving your puppy medicine, put the pill as far down his throat as you can and shove it further in with your finger until he cannot spit it out.

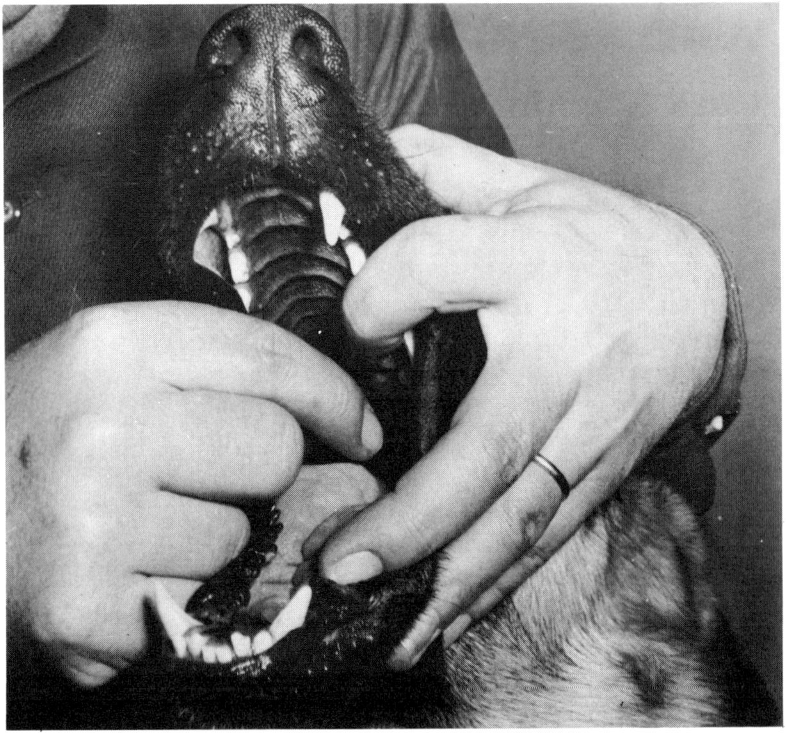

SKIN DISORDER

During the summer mostly, dogs may be afflicted with mange, eczema or fungus infections which turn their skins red in large blotches and may cause bald patches to appear. Feeding your puppy a fairly high fat diet may help prevent these from developing.

If you notice these skin conditions, check with your veterinarian immediately. Handle the dog with care as some of these conditions may be transmitted to humans. Usual treatment is to apply a salve to the puppy every day for about a month, following the treatment with a thorough washing with a mild disinfectant soap. In some severe cases, where the condition cannot be controlled, it may be necessary to destroy the puppy.

THE ANAL GLANDS

The anal glands are two small glands just inside the puppy's rectum. These glands sometimes become enlarged and must be squeezed out. Examine your puppy's rectum. If you notice a hard lump on each side of the rectum or a puffy, swollen appearance around the rectum, then the glands are swollen. In addition, the dog will usually indicate his discomfort by dragging himself along the floor, persistently licking his rectum, or rubbing his rectum against furniture or the walls of the room.

Treatment is fairly easy. To empty the glands, hold the tail in one hand, and with a piece of cleansing tissue or absorbent cotton in the other hand, apply gentle pressure on the swollen gland with the thumb and middle finger, squeezing upwards and outward. This will force the substance out of the glands.

If this is neglected, an abscess forms on either side of the rectum which will open and drain off, or it may have to be lanced and cleaned out.

WHERE TO GET MEDICAL AID

When you acquire a puppy, get the name of a reputable vet in your neighborhood and bring the puppy to him for a check-up. In many cities the Veterinarians Association arranges for a member to be on call for emergencies, nights and week ends. In most cities, the ASPCA can advise you what to do in case of an emergency. In larger cities the ASPCA or a private organization often has a mobile clinic which provides free or very low-cost veterinary service. The pet shop or kennel from which you bought your puppy will be glad to advise you on health measures and assist if an emergency occurs.

6. Housebreaking Your Puppy

Housebreaking a puppy is a long-range campaign that calls for the strategy of a Napoleon and the patience of a saint.

FIRST, PAPER TRAINING

It's almost useless to attempt to toilet train a puppy before he is at least 4 months old. Until that age, the little animal just isn't able to hold in for more than a few hours, and training is wasted. However, the paper training is the first step towards housebreaking and this can start almost the first day the puppy enters your home.

LIMIT HIS ROAMING

As soon the puppy joins your family – assuming that he's about 6 weeks old – you should start the process of paper training. Give the puppy a home of his own within your home. Set up a playpen or partition off part of a room that's going to be the puppy's domain and keep him there. If possible, use part of the kitchen for this as that's where he'll have company much of the day and won't feel all alone in the new world. Remember that he'll miss the comforting presence of the other puppies in the pet shop or kennel.

Spread several layers of newspaper over the floor of the puppy's territory. In a day or so, the puppy should normally pick one part of his section, usually a corner, for use as his toilet. When you pick up soiled papers leave a few damp pieces around so that the smell will lead him back to that spot the next time. When you find him returning to one spot, praise him. If you find him circling about or getting ready to squat in another place, pick him up and put him down in the toilet corner, praising him when he does anything. You'll be surprised how soon he'll be confining his duties to that one area, usually the most distant from the spot he chooses to sleep on.

After a few days, try removing the papers from other parts of his living quarters, just leaving in the "toilet." However, watch him carefully and whenever you anticipate any activity, pick him up and put him down on the right spot – but you'll have to act fast, and don't expect perfection for a long time.

Exercising your dog will help eliminate untimely "accidents." Bring your dog to the assigned area and praise him lavishly when he goes.

Don't rush things. Allow a few weeks for the puppy to associate paper with his functions. Then, allow him to roam around the house a bit, but always within easy range of his paper if he should need it. After each meal and after each play period, put him back on the paper. When he uses the paper make a big fuss, praising him and petting him.

When he makes a mistake, let him know by your angry voice that he is at fault, but don't make the mistake of hitting him with rolled-up newspapers or rubbing his nose in the stuff. If he makes too many mistakes off the paper, then confine him again and go through the entire paper-breaking routine again. It may be that you're rushing things a bit too much for the puppy.

As we've suggested earlier, don't be in too great a hurry to get your puppy out on the street. He's having a busy time, becoming acquainted with his new home; growing, teething, getting his shots, so the few weeks that he spends at home learning the "paper" routine are important to him.

NOW, HOUSEBREAKING

Here's the next big step toward housebreaking. When the puppy is 4 months old, some *one* member of the family should take over the job of training. It's confusing to a puppy to get commands from different people in different tones of voice.

Take the big step of picking up *all* the papers from the floor. As soon as the puppy wakes in the morning, rush him out of the house; and do that after each meal and after each hectic play period.

This Airedale puppy seems to be getting the idea. Whenever the pup seems ready to eliminate, rush him to the paper and praise him for his success.

Keep him out until something happens. When it does, be lavish with your praise. If he doesn't seem to get the idea – he may be looking for a familiar piece of paper – then put a piece of paper down outdoors for him to use. He'll soon learn that certain places outside the house have replaced the paper as the proper spot for his business, and he'll look for the gutter or grassy spot as his new place.

Try not to confuse him at this stage. One puppy we knew proudly squatted on the lawn and the family yelled at him, so he dashed back into the house and used the living room carpet, thinking that was what they wanted. It then took weeks to teach him that he was expected to do things outside the house.

CONFINE HIM

Don't give the puppy too much liberty at this stage of his housebreaking training. A dog is naturally clean and won't soil the place where he sleeps or plays, if he can help it. Tie him or keep him confined in his sleeping-playing area except when he is out for walks.

Soon, when he wants to go out, he'll whine or bark to attract your attention. When that happens, pick him up and carry him outdoors to the selected spot. Don't trust him to hold himself in while he walks out to it.

If you notice the puppy sniffing the floor while he's playing, warn him to watch his manners and take him out. The more help you can give him in avoiding mistakes, the better.

How many times a day should the puppy be walked? That depends on the puppy, his diet, and his digestive system. As a minimum, he should be walked the first thing in the morning, after every meal, after every period of hard play, any time he seems to be asking to be walked (there will be a lot of false alarms), and the last thing at night.

NIGHTTIME TRAINING

Nighttime training during the housebreaking period depends on how much you value your sleep. If you want to spend a quiet night, then use papers for a while at night, leaving them down where the puppy can reach them. He should be tied on a long leash or cord that will allow him to sleep comfortably and to walk over to the paper when he needs to.

However, if housebreaking the puppy means more to you than sleep, then tie the puppy with a short lead to his sleeping quarters. When he has to do something, he'll wake you up rather than soil his bed. But after a few weeks, he should be able to keep himself in until morning, especially if you help by cutting down on the amount of liquid in his late meal. It helps, too, if you make the late walk really late and plop him right into his sleeping place after that walk.

CORRECTING MISTAKES

Mistakes are bound to happen. Sometimes they will be the puppy's fault, sometimes they will be yours, but blame the puppy anyway. If you catch him immediately after a mistake, correct him promptly. If you don't notice it until much later, then skip it. The dog won't connect the correction with something that happened a long time ago.

When you find evidence of a fresh mistake or catch him in the act, take him firmly by the collar and march him over to the scene of the crime. Reprimand him in an angry tone of voice and slap him sharply on the rump. Then take him outside and, if he does anything, praise him and pet him. Remember that in training a dog the animal won't resent being punished for something if he understands why he is being punished, especially if he is praised when he does something well.

You can make housebreaking easier if you set a routine and keep to it. Feed the puppy at regular hours, and try to arrange his last daily meal at about 5 or 6 in the evening.

This dog certainly appreciates the convenience of being able to let himself in and out when the necessity arrives!

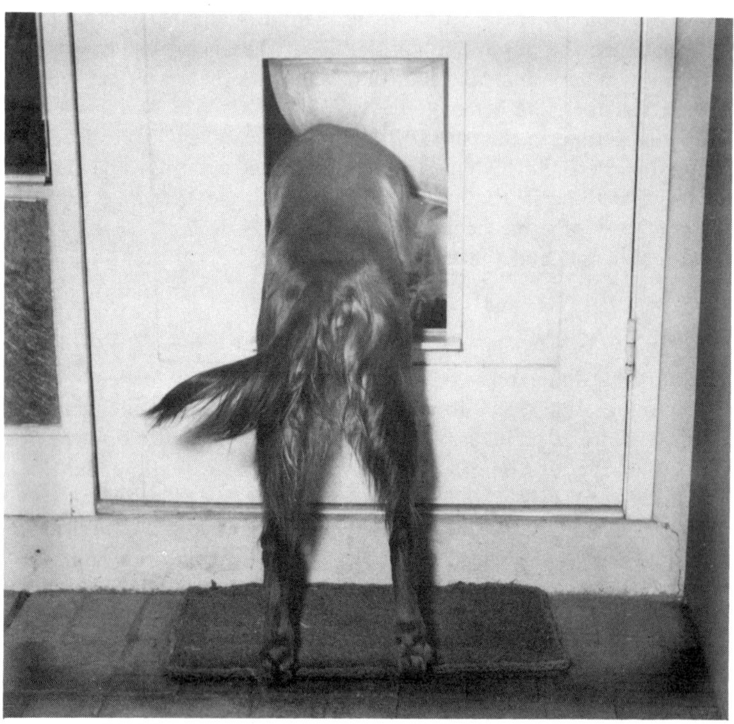

This Pug has been supplied with his own personal hydrant. This wooden fireplug helps both the dog and people associate which area has been set aside for the dog's use.

CURB TRAINING

City dogs must be trained to obey the signs which read: "Curb Your Dog" and often "$25 Fine for Violation."

Teaching the dog to do his business on leash and where you want him to is not difficult if you use some patience. Normally, a dog likes to roam around until he finds a satisfactory spot. However, curb training can be accomplished in a week or so with the average dog of about 4 months of age.

As for housebreaking, keep the puppy tied close to his sleeping quarters during the night. First thing in the morning, take him down to the street – it's better to carry him – put him down in the gutter and walk him back and forth. Usually the dog will make a puddle and then will sniff about, investigating the street. If nothing else happens, after about 15 minutes take the puppy back into the house and tie him or confine him to his sleeping quarters. Do not let him run around the house. Try again a while later. Sooner or later, the puppy will do his stuff in the gutter. Then praise him, pet him.

A partition across the kitchen doorway is ideal to keep your puppy confined while he's learning house manners and still let him see what's going on in the family.

While doing this, use some word that the puppy will learn to associate with the purpose of his trip to the gutter. In a few weeks the puppy will learn the meaning of the command and it will help when you take him to some strange place and want him to cooperate.

It is usually a bit harder to train a male puppy to confine his activities to the area you select than it is to train a female, and the older the puppy the longer it may take to get the idea across. In the early stages of curb training, it's also a good idea to carry a pocketful of cleansing tissue or paper napkins to clean up any public mistakes the puppy may make.

Some dog trainers use a glycerine suppository to speed up the dog's action for the first day or two of curb training. You can try that if your puppy turns out to be a curb-problem child.

7. Training Your Puppy

Training your puppy to be a civilized member of the community is your third responsibility as a dog owner. Dog training is fairly easy because most dogs seem to have instinctive desires to do what their owners want them to do. Unlike other animals who learn because they find that something unpleasant will happen if they do not obey, dogs seem to enjoy cooperating with their owners.

The big problem, however, is communicating with the puppy and showing him what you expect of him. For instance, telling your puppy, "I want you to sit here and keep quiet" doesn't mean anything to the little animal even if you repeat it twenty times in a loud and angry tone of voice.

A dog can learn to associate a limited number of words with the response that is expected of him. The first word in your puppy's vocabulary should be "No." Tone of voice is important in training a puppy and the first time your puppy misbehaves or grabs something he shouldn't, use the word "No" in a firm, angry tone of voice. If necessary, accompany it with a sharp slap on the puppy's nose.

SPARING THE ROD

Most people who have never owned a dog say you should never hit a puppy. A gentle slap on the nose will help a puppy learn, but never hit a puppy in anger. Never call the dog to you and then hit him, and don't make the mistake of chasing him, waving a folded newspaper or a ruler at him. When you have to punish the puppy, hold him firmly and give him one sharp slap. Then shortly afterwards make friends with him and show him that you don't really hate him and that he is forgiven.

SOME PRINCIPLES OF DOG TRAINING

Puppies learn through association. A puppy will be amazingly quick to connect his acts with the results they produce. For example, a puppy finds out that if he plays with a rubber toy he is praised; if he plays with a slipper, he is corrected. Very soon he'll learn what he should do and what he shouldn't – if the owner will only show him.

A correction must be applied immediately to be effective. Discipline

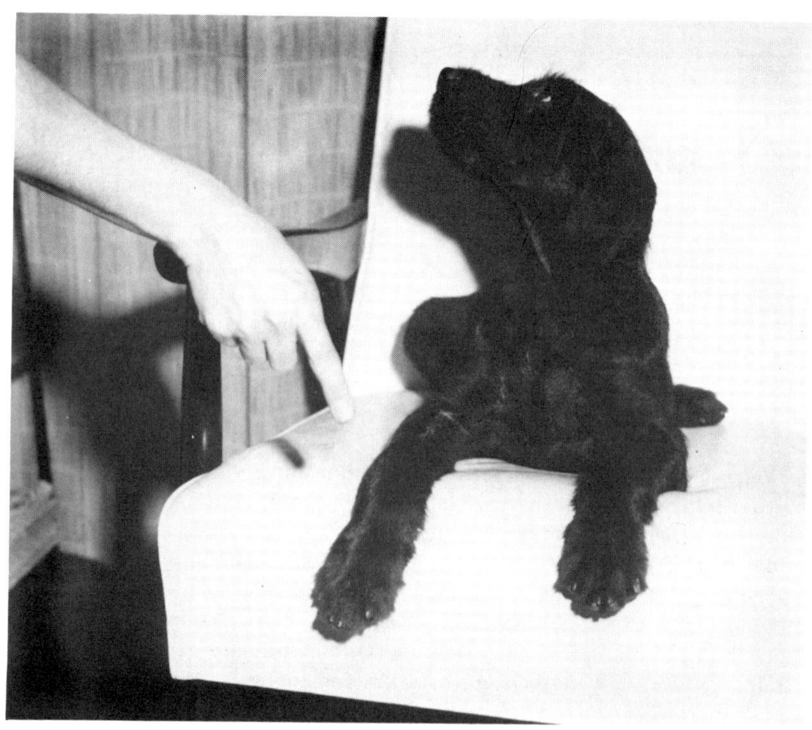

If you snould find your puppy on the furniture, immediately reprimand and remove him. A sharp "no!" should be sufficient to show your disapproval.

the puppy the instant he does something wrong. A young puppy has a short memory span. Corrections applied a length of time after the offense are wasted and only confuse the animal.

Training must be consistent. Correct the puppy each time he makes a mistake. He'll be confused if he is allowed to do something once and is punished for doing the same thing another time.

Match the training to the puppy's disposition. You'll soon find out whether your puppy is shy or strong-willed; how he reacts to criticism; whether he learns quickly or slowly.

BASIC TRAINING

As soon as you get your puppy you can begin to train him. When you put out his food dish always use the same word to call him, whether it's "Food," "Dinner," "Eats," or any word you prefer. Use the dog's name consistently so that he'll learn who he is, and alway use the same name. If the puppy is saddled with a fancy name like Herman Van Clunkenhorn of Van Dam Corners, give him some simple nickname that he can learn to respond to.

The simpler commands to "Come," "Sit" and "Lie down" can be learned by even very young puppies. Let your puppy connect the word "come" with a reward of food and he'll gallop over every time he hears that command. Always use his name first to get his attention, then use the word of command.

Note of caution: Never ask the puppy to come when you want to correct or discipline him. And if you say "Come" and nothing happens, don't punish the puppy. The word "Come" must have a pleasant meaning to the dog and even one incident that may associate "Come" with anything unrewarding can set back the training program.

MEET THE COLLAR AND LEASH

Make your puppy's introduction to the collar and leash a painless meeting. When you buy a collar be certain that it is loose enough to be comfortable and not so loose that the puppy can back up and slide his head through it. Let the puppy wear the collar and dangle the leash for a while. He can play with this new equipment until he gets used to the feel of the collar around his neck.

For even the smaller puppies, a collar and leash is preferable to a shoulder harness for training purposes.

At first, pull gently on the leash and take short walks around the room to give the puppy some idea of what walking on a lead is like.

Don't let the first real outdoor walk turn into a tug of war. Most young puppies are better at coming than going, so carry the puppy a short distance away from home. Then put him down, pat your knee, say "Come" and start walking. The idea of training with the leash is to use sharp tugs and then hold the leash slack when the puppy responds, not to drag the little thing along. However, many puppies will just plant their rear ends on the ground and refuse to budge. If that happens, jerk the leash sharply. When the puppy gets up on his feet, praise him and start walking.

Note of warning: Carry some clean-up materials with you. The puppy may get a little excited during his first walking sessions and make mistakes on the sidewalk.

"SIT" AND "LIE DOWN"

Even before he's old enough to leave the house, the young puppy can be taught to respond to the commands "Sit" and "Lie Down." This training is not just to teach him tricks, but is the beginning of an under-

It's fun to walk a well-trained dog, but keep your puppy on leash until he's old enough to be trusted not to scamper away.

standing between the puppy and his owner. Even a young puppy seems to get a big kick out of doing things for his master.

In this early training, don't depend too much on tidbits or other food rewards to get your puppy to respond. Any dog will work eagerly just to be praised and petted in return.

To teach the puppy to sit, just hold his head high, using the leash, and press down on his hindquarters while repeating the word "Sit." When he begins to get the idea, keep him sitting for a few seconds before praising him, as the normal response to praise is to jump up for more attention. Once he begins to respond properly, don't overdo the sitting commands, and keep the training more like a game than a lesson.

Try giving the command to sit when you take him outdoors or when you go visiting, and when you take him for a ride in the family car, and always praise the puppy for good response.

Teaching to "Lie Down" should be done with the puppy on leash so that he can't follow his natural impulse to dash away. First tell the puppy to sit, then pull his front feet forward from underneath and press on his back to force him down. Hold him down, repeating the command "Down," or "Lie Down." He'll probably struggle to get up the first few times, but sooner or later he'll get the idea and drop down on the verbal command.

When he's lying down, don't praise or pet him, but tell him in a low voice that he's a good puppy and scratch his ears or stroke his head.

If you find that you're getting no response whatever to your efforts to teach your puppy to sit or lie down, try again in a few weeks; your puppy may still be too young for this step in his training.

TEACH HIM TO STAY ALONE

The plight of the dog owner who has to find a dog sitter to keep his pet company for a day or even for an evening is usually the result of poor puppy training.

This dog a top obedience contender, a product of hard work by both master and dog. He is shown taking the hurdle jump after retrieving a wooden dumbell for his owner.

A puppy can be trained to stay by himself without tearing up the house or keeping the neighbors awake with his barking, and this training can begin when the puppy is 8 to 10 weeks old. In the beginning, let the puppy become accustomed to being left alone. Leave some toys or playthings in his playpen or in the corner of the room where he lives. At first he'll howl in frustration and anger, but when he finds that it doesn't do any good, he'll quiet down. Try this training in the daytime for the sake of the neighbors.

The next step should be taken when the puppy is well enough housebroken to have the run of his room. Shut the door of the room in which the puppy is staying. As soon as he barks, rap loudly on the door and shout, "No. Stop that!" If the barking persists, then go into the room, take the culprit by the collar and cuff him sharply. If you have to repeat the lesson, be a bit firmer with the correction each time.

This may turn into a battle of wills with the puppy, but you can win. Sometimes the puppy will soil the floor to teach you a lesson or will deliberately damage something in the room. When that happens it's up to you to show him who is boss. This is an important point in training and one that you must win for an enjoyable future dog-person relationship.

Some puppies will keep quiet when they know that a person is in the house or apartment, but will blow the roof off when alone. Here you have to use strategy and fool the dog into thinking you have gone away. Go to the outside door, slam it and wait for results. If you hear barking, slam hard on the door and tell the puppy off, but good. If you have to go into the room to shut him up, give him a little lesson that he won't forget soon.

Remember, in this part of training you are working against a dog's instinct to sound off and it takes a lot of work and patience. It's really worth it to train a dog that can be left alone for hours with no worries about indignant neighbors, lease-canceling landlords or damaged house furnishings.

WATCHDOG OR NOT?

It's up to you to decide whether you want your puppy to grow into a watchdog that barks at the approach of any person to your home or a dog that quietly minds his own business. At an early age, your puppy will growl or bark at the approach of a stranger. If you want to train a watchdog, praise the dog for this each time he repeats the performance. If you don't want a watchdog, just say "No!" and indicate your displeasure at the barking at strange people.

But, above all, be consistent. Don't praise the dog for barking at a peddler and bawl him out for barking at Aunt Agatha.

If the puppy does not respond to verbal orders to cease barking, place your hands around his muzzle and hold the jaws together, while saying "No!" If the puppy continues to try to bark, slap him on the nose. Most dogs dislike loud noises, so try dropping a large book on the floor or banging anything if your puppy barks when you tell him to stop.

This no-barking training will be helped if you place your puppy on leash when you know someone is coming, so that you can correct him as soon as he begins to bark. Many dogs precede their barking with a throat rumble so you can try to grab your puppy's muzzle before the bark comes out and stop it, whenever you hear that pre-barking sound.

SHOES AREN'T TOYS

Your puppy will destroy things around the house. That's one of the perils of owning a puppy. You can expect to find corners of cushions and carpets chewed, slippers and shoes gnawed, clothing damaged – anything the puppy can reach. Some experts say it's because the puppy is teething, others because he is just bored, still others just blame it on puppyhood.

You can reduce the possibility of damage by keeping things out of the puppy's reach until he gets the idea of private property into his head. Provide the puppy with his own chewing toys. You can find a selection at your pet shop, but make sure they are not made of soft rubber which the puppy can chew up and swallow. And don't make the mistake of giving him an old slipper or glove to play with, or he'll think that all shoes and gloves are toys.

This puppy may look cute nestled in this slipper, but be careful not to let them chew. Shoes are common targets for puppy chewing.

When training your dog to sit, place your hand on the dog's rump and exert just enough pressure to get the dog down into the correct sitting position.

When the puppy has been left alone, he will often act guilty if he has damaged anything. Lead him over to the damaged object – you'll probably have to drag him over – and give him a good bawling out.

If the older puppy, who should know better, damages anything, he's probably doing it out of spite and should be corrected with firmness.

JUMPING ON PEOPLE

Puppies like to jump up on people, but at the age of 3 or 4 months, you should begin teaching your puppy – especially if he is of a larger breed – that this is not acceptable behavior.

Every time the puppy tries to jump up on anyone, push him down and say "No!" Be consistent in this. In addition, make sure that your friends and relatives react the same way when the puppy tries to jump up on them. A puppy can show that he likes people by tail-wagging and hand-licking, without jumping up on them. If words are not sufficient, try sterner measures. When he jumps up, raise your knee and knock the puppy backwards.

However, temper this treatment with friendship. After each correction, pat the puppy so he'll know that people don't hate him. Another trick is to command the puppy to sit when anyone approaches and to keep him sitting until the enthusiasm of the greeting has begun to wear off.

KEEPING OFF FURNITURE

Let's face it. An upholstered piece of furniture or a bed is more comfortable than a spot on the floor or even on the carpet, and any intelligent puppy soon discovers that fact. Some families surrender an older chair or sofa to the puppy and that's one solution. However, a puppy can be trained to keep off furniture.

First try using "NO" every time the puppy goes where he isn't wanted. Many puppies will respect the owner's wishes so long as he is around, but the minute the owner is out, up goes the puppy on the furniture.

There are a number of ways to work on that part of puppy discipline. Sometimes spreading plastic on the furniture will discourage the puppy. Another stunt that often works is to set a small mousetrap on the dog's forbidden resting spot. Dog goes up, trap goes off, dog goes down and stays down. If the small trap catches the dog's fur or paw it won't do any damage.

Before blaming the dog for climbing on furniture, look over the sleeping place you have set up for him. Many dogs climb up on furniture because the corner where they are supposed to stay is in a draft or in a location that the dog doesn't like.

TEACHING STREET BEHAVIOR

Automobiles are a dog's worst enemy. Car accidents rate as one of the leading causes of dog fatalities, and one of the best things you can do for your puppy is to teach him from the start that roads are dangerous. The first time he tries to dash into the street, pull him back and show him firmly that a road is no place for him.

A puppy can be trained to stay in a yard if he finds out that straying beyond his boundaries means that unpleasant things happen to him. How-

The dog that's allowed to roam on the street isn't a good insurance risk. Train your puppy to stay away from cars or he'll endanger not only his own life but human life as drivers swerve to avoid him.

ever, keep in mind that a male dog is somewhat more liable to wander off than a female; that some breeds (such as retrievers) are more likely to go off on their own.

A fenced yard is the safest for a puppy, but he should be watched carefully until he is old enough to be trusted to stay in his own yard.

Most puppies will become excited when they meet another dog, but if you have been training yours to sit on command he should stay at your side without tugging at the leash and trying to get away.

Another word of warning: Don't be in too much of a hurry to show how your puppy walks around off-leash with you. Until a dog is a year or so old, he is just too young to be fully dependable, and should be kept leashed whenever you take him out.

8. Showing Your Puppy

If you have made the additional investment that brought you a purebred puppy, you may have an idea in back of your mind that you'd like to enter him in dog shows with the hope of winning blue ribbons and trophies. But before the puppy can be entered in a show, he must be registered with the American Kennel Club or must be eligible for registration. (See Chapter 2.)

A puppy must be at least 6 months old before he can be shown. But before going to the expense of entering a show, it's always good to get the opinion of some experts first to see whether he measures up to present-day standards for his breed. Have some experienced breeder or kennel owner give you a frank opinion on the puppy's chances – although even experts are often baffled by the decisions of the judges. Also, you should get the T.F.H. book on your puppy's breed, to see how he matches up against the color pictures of the breed champions you'll find on its pages.

SANCTIONED MATCHES

Sanctioned matches – informal shows held by local kennel clubs or breed specialty clubs – are a good way to get show ring experience for yourself and your puppy. These shows are usually held during week ends or in the evening and the entry fee is seldom more than $1. You can win ribbons and small trophies at these matches and you'll get the feel of showing your dog and seeing how he rates against the competition.

In the puppy classes, the judges aren't too strict about the young dogs' ring behavior, but your puppy should be trained to show his gaits by trotting alongside you at the judge's command – on leash and running around the ring with other dogs and handlers without becoming too excited. In addition, the puppy should stand still while the judge looks him over and runs his hands over his body to check his flesh and his conformation. For best results, he must be taught to stand in such a way that he will be showing his best points to the judge and the dog show audience.

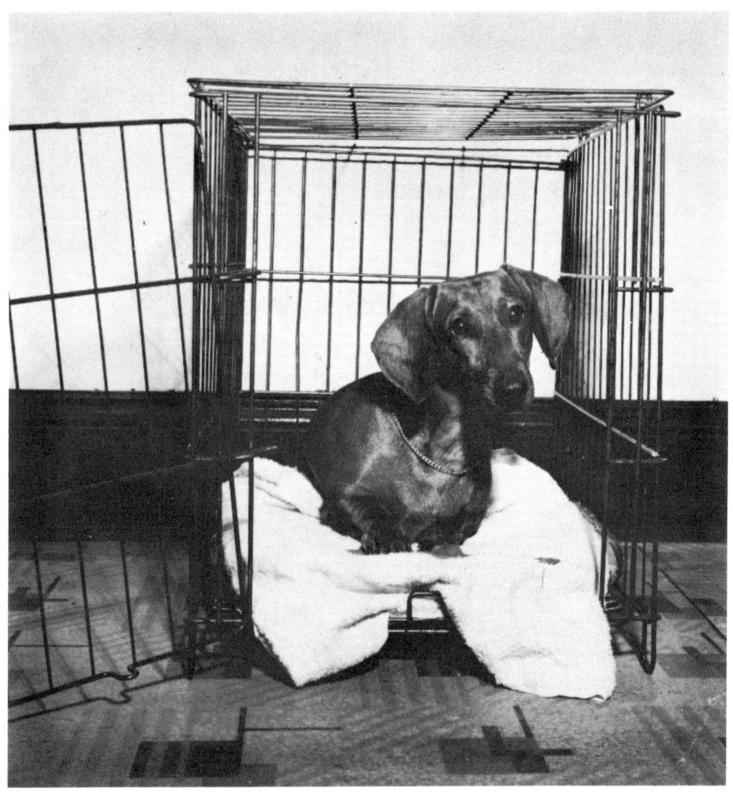

If you own a purebred puppy, small dog variety, and plan to enter him into competitions, you will find that this cage is a necessity at competitons that require the presence of your dog overnight.

DOG SHOWS

The formal dog shows conducted under A.K.C. auspices will give your puppy an opportunity to begin earning points toward his championship. Entries for these shows have to be made in advance. If you write to the Foley Dog Show Organization, 2009 Ranstead Street, Philadelphia, Pennsylvania, they'll put you on the mailing list to receive notices of dog shows in your part of the country. They'll also send on request a free booklet "Rules Applying to Registration and Dog Shows" that will fill you in on the technical details involved in a dog show.

Before entering your puppy in a show, try to visit one or two shows as a spectator so that you'll see how the show is conducted. Grooming is important and the "show" cut is required of some breeds. Dogs are judged basically on how close they come to the standards of physical perfection of their breed and the undefinable standard of "personality" which is different in every breed.

OBEDIENCE COMPETITION

Most dog shows also offer obedience classes in which dogs compete for prizes and for scores that will qualify them for the different obedience degrees that we mentioned when we discussed pedigrees. There are no special puppy classes in obedience competition, although an occasional dog "genius" will take an obedience degree when he is only a bit past 6 months of age.

If you are interested in obedience work with your puppy – training usually starts when the dog is about 8 or 9 months old – you'll find much information in the T.F.H. book, "How To Housebreak and Train Your Dog."

This champion Collie pup displays its well-earned ribbons.

9. Breeding and Caring for Newborn Puppies

If you have a female dog, you may intend to breed her, or nature may take care of things and you'll find yourself with an approaching litter of pups.

PLANNED BREEDING

It is best not to breed your female dog until the second or third time that she comes into heat. As an amateur breeder, the chances of making any money on a litter of dogs are pretty slight. As a matter of fact, most persons who find themselves with a litter of pups have trouble finding homes for them even if they want to give away some of the dogs. And plan on running into some expenses. You'll probably have veterinarian fees. Chances are you'll have to pay for the puppies' first innoculations and for having their tails docked and ears trimmed, if the breed calls for that treatment. In addition, taking care of a mother dog and a litter of puppies takes considerable time.

On the other side of the ledger, watching a mother dog and a litter of pups is an enlightening experience – and wonderful for the children in your family!

The dog's gestation period is about 9 weeks, so plan ahead. Figure about 6 weeks after birth before the puppies can leave their mother so that you'll have puppies available about 15 weeks from the time of mating. If you can offer puppies about Christmas time or in the spring you'll have a better chance of disposing of them.

SELECTING THE FATHER

If you are mating a purebred bitch with the hope of producing show prospects, try to get a dog whose pedigree can match that of your female. If you can find one with several champions in his background and some ancestors in common with your dog, you may produce winning combinations. Also seek a dog whose good points may overcome any deficiencies of yours, and vice versa. If the male has a good show record, so much thc better.

In usual practice, the owner of the female pays a stud fee which is set by the owner of the male. A litter is not guaranteed, but you are usually given the right to another mating if the first does not produce. Sometimes the owner of the male will agree to take his choice of the litter in place of a stud fee. But make all agreements in writing to avoid future disputes. In many of the dog magazines you'll find advertisements for printed stud-contracts which cover all eventualities.

If you are just mating your dog for puppies and for fun, then try to select a male with a pleasant disposition to assure that the puppies will make good pets. In such cases, the owner of the male will usually settle for one of the puppies as the stud fee.

BUILD UP THE FEMALE

Giving birth is a strain on the dog and she should be built up to prepare for the experience. First, make sure that she is in good health and free of any skin diseases or worms which could be passed on to the puppies. Starting some weeks before the breeding, put her on a rich vitamin and high calcium diet. Some veterinarians suggest re-inoculating the female against distemper and hepatitis before the puppies are born so that they will receive some immunity against these diseases at birth.

WHEN TO MATE

Your female should be ready to be mated about 12 days after the first colored discharge appears. For some reason, it is often more satisfactory to have the mating take place at the male's home, so try to make arrangements to leave her with the owner of the male for a few days, although you can take her to be mated and bring her home immediately afterwards. Some breeders suggest two matings a few days apart. If you are not experienced in breeding dogs, you should seek the advice of an experienced breeder or of your veterinarian.

THE NINE WEEKS

During the time that thc female is carrying the pups, there is little that you have to do. Just see that your female receives her usual food with added vitamins and mineral supplements. Her appetite will increase as the weeks pass, so feed her as much as she'll eat. However, during the last two weeks she will probably lose her appetite. Also, during the last few weeks, as the mother grows heavier, restrain her from jumping or other violent exercise.

GET READY FOR THE PUPPIES

A few days before you expect the puppies, prepare a whelping box; its size will depend on the size of your dog. A large, square box with walls

These Beagle puppies are almost ready to be weaned. They look so sleek and healthy, there should be no problem of selling or finding good homes for them.

high enough will keep the puppies confined; leave one side low enough to let the mother get out. Lay in a stock of newspapers because you'll want a thick, absorbent layer of newspaper underfoot, and you'll be changing the papers frequently. For the first few days after birth you should spread an old blanket or quilt over the papers.

SIGNS OF APPROACHING BIRTH

Ordinarily, a few days before giving birth, the female will show signs of restlessness. She'll refuse food, tear the papers in her bed, seem to be making a sort of nest for herelf. The real test is the dog's temperature, which will fall to 100° about 12 hours before whelping. Check her temperature twice daily and be ready for action when the temperature falls below the normal 102°.

HOSPITAL VS. HOME BIRTH

A dog's instincts will usually guide her through the process of giving birth. However, if you feel squeamish or worried, it might be best to take her to the veterinarian and let her give birth there. Chances are that you'll call the vet anyway, so it might be better to arrange in advance for hospital delivery.

When the first puppy is born, the mother should break the membrane enclosing it and start to lick the puppy dry. You can help dry with a soft bath towel. The afterbirth will follow the birth of each puppy, attached to the puppy by the umbilical cord. The mother will probably eat the afterbirth after biting the cord; but it's better to remove them after the first one or two. Also remove the wet newspapers to help the mother keep the pen clean.

If the mother fails to bite the umbilical cord, or bites it too close to the body, you should take over the job. You can tear the cord, or cut it with a sawing motion of sterilized scissors, about 2 inches from the body. Then dip the end of the cord in a shallow dish of iodine. In a few days, the cord will dry up and fall off.

Puppies should follow each other at intervals of about a half hour. If you feel sure there are more to come and there is a delay, take the dog outside for a short, brisk walk which may induce labor to start again.

If the mother seems to be straining without producing a puppy, she may be having trouble with an upside-down or "breech" delivery. Try to help straighten the puppy, if you feel you can, using a well-soaped finger, but don't attempt to force it out. Better still, call the veterinarian. If necessary, he can give a hormone injection which will speed delivery.

FIRST AID FOR THE NEW PUPS

As soon as each puppy is dry, you can help by holding him up to a nipple for his first meal. Then put him back in the pen, but out of the mother's way while she is still whelping. If you have a large litter, prepare emergency supplies of evaporated milk, corn syrup, a little water and egg yolk. This should be warmed and can be fed from a baby bottle. Watch especially for the "shrimps" of the litter who may not be getting enough food because the larger pups may keep them away from the nipples.

In cold weather, place an electric heating pad in the pen to provide warmth for the mother and pups. If the mother seems to resent your interference then let her handle things her own way.

At first, the mother will nurse the pups lying down, later from a standing position. When the pups are about 2 weeks old, their eyes should open and they should be ready to begin lapping food from a dish. By the time the pups are 5 weeks' old, they should be fully weaned. As with babies, give them semi-solid foods at first, starting with baby cereal and working up to baby meats and then finely ground chopped meat. At about a month of age, they should be starting on their regular baby dog diets described in Chapter 3 of this book.

Pups are sloppy little eaters so you might help keep them clean by sponging them off after meals.

The veterinarian should see the pups during their first month to check them for worms, give them their first puppy shots and just look them over generally. If they need tail- or ear-clipping, arrange with the vet for that treatment in advance and have the whole litter done at the same time. It's a good idea to get a note from the veterinarian telling what shots and treatments the puppies have received so that those who take the puppies can pass the information on to their own veterinarian.

Provide a whelping box in an out-of-the-way corner for the dog who is about to become a mother. Line the box with many layers of newspaper and add an old quilt or blanket so your dog will be as comfortable as possible, like this Miniature Schnauzer.

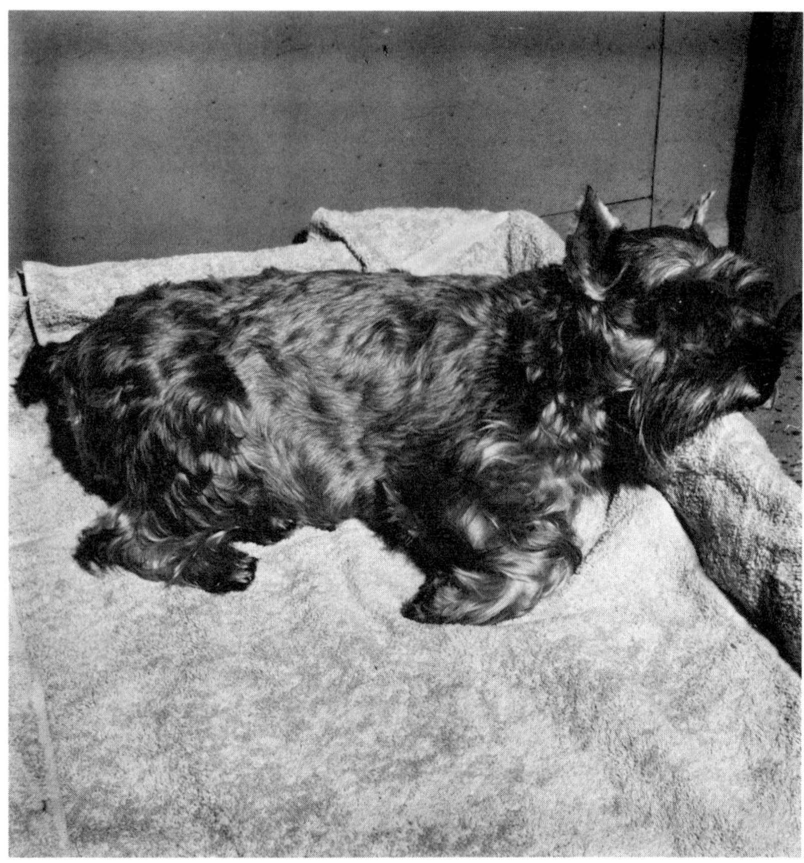